ACCOUNTING LIFEPA

FINANCIAL STATEME
FOR A PROPRIETORSHIP

CONTENTS

Author: Daniel L. Ritzman, B.S.

Editors: Alan Christopherson, M.S.
Jennifer L. Davis, B.S.

Alpha Omega Publications®

804 N. 2nd Ave. E., Rock Rapids, IA 51246-1759
© MM by Alpha Omega Publications, Inc.   All rights reserved.
LIFEPAC is a registered trademark of Alpha Omega Publications, Inc.

ACCOUNTING LIFEPAC 6
FINANCIAL STATEMENTS

OVERVIEW

The fifth step in the accounting cycle is to prepare financial statements at the end of the accounting period. Financial statements assist owners and managers in making business decisions. These financial statements include the income statement, the equity statement and the balance sheet. These statements should present all financial information in an understandable manner in order to provide a clear and informative picture of the financial condition of the business.

In LIFEPAC 5 you learned about a very important tool that accountants use to organize this financial information prior to preparing financial statements—the worksheet. In this LIFEPAC® you will learn how to use the worksheet to prepare the income statement, the equity statement and the balance sheet.

OBJECTIVES

When you have completed this LIFEPAC you will be able to:

1. Define the accounting terms associated with the preparation of all financial statements.

2. Recognize accounting concepts and practices associated with a worksheet and financial statements for a service business.

3. Prepare an income statement for a service business organized as a sole proprietorship.

4. Prepare an equity statement for a service business organized as a sole proprietorship.

5. Prepare a balance sheet illustrating the financial condition of a service business organized as a sole proprietorship.

VOCABULARY

Account Format – a balance sheet format that lists the assets on the left and the liabilities and equity on the right, similar to the accounting equation.

Balance Sheet – a financial statement that reports assets, liabilities and owner's equity on a specific date.

Fiscal Period – the length of the accounting cycle for which a business summarizes and reports financial information.

Income Statement – a financial statement that reports the revenue and expenses for a fiscal period.

Net – the amount remaining after all deductions have been made.

Net Income – the difference between total revenue and total expenses when total revenue is greater than total expenses.

Net Loss – the difference between total revenue and total expenses when total expenses are greater than total revenue.

Report Format – the most common balance sheet format, with the asset section listed first, followed by the liability and equity sections. This is a two-column report similar to the income statement.

Statement of Owner's Equity – the financial statement that reports the changes in capital that have occurred between the beginning and ending of a given fiscal period.

Worksheet – a columnar accounting form used to summarize the general ledger information needed to prepare financial statements.

SECTION I. THE INCOME STATEMENT

Introduction

One of the most important functions of the accounting system is to accurately report the profitability of a business. This accountability is achieved by comparing concrete facts and figures. From the objective evidence provided, the profitability of the business can be determined. As an example, a business purchases an item for $200.00 and sells it for $250.00. After recording this business transaction, the accountant has the objective evidence to show a net income of $50.00 for this item. Thus, by using the accounting concept of objective evidence, a formula has been created for determining business profit.

Any business organized today is created with the expectation of making a profit. Profit, or net income, is the main factor that indicates a business has reached this primary goal. For every firm, big or small, a profitable operation is necessary for survival in our free enterprise system. A profitable operation not only increases the owner's equity but also increases total assets. From the basic accounting equation (A = L + C), we have established that any change in an asset due to daily business operations (sale of a product or service or borrowing money from a bank) also must change another asset, a liability, or the owner's equity (capital). Also, any portion of the profit from business operations may be kept by the business for expansion. A profit retained is usually spent for new equipment, new research, or expanding sales territories. It is important many times to retain some of the profit to maintain a growing company.

Many people in the financial world feel that the income statement is the most important business statement. This statement indicates if the business has reached its primary goal—generating a profit from operations. An **income statement** is sometimes referred to as *a statement of profit and loss, a statement of revenue and expenses, a statement of earnings*, or *a statement of operations*. It reports all financial information gathered over a specific period of time to determine if a business has earned a net income or produced a net loss for that accounting period. A **net income** is earned when the revenue for the fiscal period exceeds expenses for the same period. A **net loss** occurs when the expenses for the fiscal period exceed the revenue earned for the same period.

The Worksheet. The worksheet is the basis for the preparation of the formal income statement. The eight-column worksheet shown below organizes financial information into four sections:

Lawson's Lawn Care

Worksheet

For the Month Ended July 31, 20—

| | 1 | | 2 | | 3 | | 4 | |
| | TRIAL BALANCE | | ADJUSTMENTS | | INCOME STATEMENT | | BALANCE SHEET | |
ACCOUNT TITLE	DEBIT	CREDIT	DEBIT	CREDIT	DEBIT	CREDIT	DEBIT	CREDIT
Cash	7822 00						7822 00	
Petty Cash	300 00						300 00	
Supplies	4319 00			(a) 1341 00			2978 00	
Prepaid Insurance	1600 00			(b) 330 00			1270 00	
John's Garage		1630 00						1630 00
Wick Supplies		300 00						300 00
D. Lawson, Capital		9000 00						9000 00
D. Lawson, Drawing	500 00						500 00	
Sales		4367 00				4367 00		
Advertising Expense	86 00				86 00			
Insurance Expense			(b) 330 00		330 00			
Miscellaneous Expense	95 00				95 00			
Rent Expense	450 00				450 00			
Supplies Expense			(a) 1341 00		1341 00			
Utilities Expense	125 00				125 00			
Totals	15297 00	15297 00	1671 00	1671 00	2427 00	4367 00	12870 00	10930 00
Net Income					1940 00			1940 00
					4367 00	4367 00	12870 00	12870 00

1. The *trial balance* section proves the equality of the debits and credits in the ledger. This section of the worksheet is used to create the formal trial balance which you have already studied in LIFEPAC 4.

2. The *adjustments* section is used to update the balances of accounts such as Supplies and Prepaid Insurance. The balances of these accounts at the end of the fiscal period do not

accurately reflect the changes that have occurred due to the daily internal operations of the business. Supplies that were purchased at the beginning of the fiscal period are not used up until a future fiscal period. Since insurance is usually paid for a year in advance, the unexpired insurance must be carried over as an asset for the next accounting cycle. The costs incurred in the operation of a business are expenses, and adjustments must be made to transfer these costs to the proper expense account.

3. The *income statement* section contains the updated balances of all revenue and expense accounts and is used to calculate net income or net loss.

4. The *balance sheet* section contains the permanent accounts of the business and provides all the necessary information to prepare the formal balance sheet and the formal income statement.

Purpose of the Income Statement. The income statement provides the following information:

1. The accounting period (fiscal period) covered by the statement,

2. A summary of all sources of revenue for the fiscal period,

3. All expenses that are matched against the revenue for the period, and

4. The net income or net loss for the fiscal period.

Since an income statement is a part of the permanent and official records of a business, it is prepared in ink. It can be typed, prepared by computer, or handwritten. Since it will be scrutinized by managers, owners, and outside businessmen such as creditors, it is important that it be prepared accurately and neatly.

The Heading Section

Any financial statement heading must include three elements:

1. *Who* – the name of the business;

2. *What* – the name of the statement; and

3. *When* – the date of the statement.

1	Lawson's Lawn Care
2	Income Statement
3	For the Month Ended July 31, 20—

The date of the statement reflects the ending date of the current fiscal period. The heading above indicates that the fiscal period for Lawson's Lawn Care is one month. Fiscal periods can vary in length—one month, three months, a calendar year (January to December) or a fiscal year (the last day of a twelve-month period).

- A 3-month fiscal period: "For the Quarter Ended July 31, 20—"
- A calendar year: "For the Year Ended December 31, 20—"
- A fiscal year: "For the Year Ended July 31, 20—"

The Revenue Section

The information to complete this section is found in the worksheet's account title section and the income statement section's credit column. Remember that revenue accounts always have credit balances and will, therefore, be listed in the credit column of the income statement section of the worksheet.

Steps for preparing the revenue section:

4. Write the classification "Revenue" on the first line against the left margin.

5. Write the account title for the revenue account on the second line, indented about five spaces.

6. Write the account balance in the second money column of the income statement. This balance is found in the income statement credit column on the worksheet. Since Lawson's Lawn Care has only one source of revenue there is no need to total the revenue section.

Lawson's Lawn Care			
Income Statement			
For the Month Ended July 31, 20—			
Revenue: **4**			
Sales **5**			64367 00

The Expense Section

After completing the revenue section of an income statement, it is necessary to enter the expenses for the fiscal period. Again, the account titles are found in the worksheet's account title column. The account balances are found in the income statement section's debit column. Expenses have debit balances and are listed in the debit column of the income statement section of the worksheet.

Steps for preparing the expense section:

7. Write the classification "Expenses" on the line following the revenue totals against the left margin.

8. Write the account titles for the expense accounts underneath the classification "Expenses." Indent the account titles about five spaces.

9. Write the account balances in the first money column of the income statement. These balances are found in the income statement debit column on the worksheet.

10. Draw a single line under the last expense amount in the first column.

11. Indent the words "Total Expenses" so they appear under the last listed expense account.

12. Total the balances of all the expense accounts, and write the total in the second column on the same line as the words "Total Expenses."

NOTE: The income statement contains two balance or money columns which are neither debit nor credit columns, but are used as *list* columns and *totals* columns. The first money column is used to list account balances, and the second money column is used for totals.

Lawson's Lawn Care
Income Statement
For the Month Ended July 31, 20—

Revenue:				
Sales			4367	00
Expenses: 7				
8 Advertising Expense	9 86	00		
Insurance Expense	330	00		
Miscellaneous Expense	95	00		
Rent Expense	450	00		
Supplies Expense	1341	00		
Utilities Expense	10 125	00		
11 Total Expenses			12 2427	00

Calculating Net Income or Net Loss

Steps for determining net income or net loss:

13. Rule a single line under the total expense amount in the second column.

14. Subtract the total expenses from the total revenue to determine the net income. Enter the amount of the net income in the second column under the amount representing total expenses.

15. Write the words "Net Income" (or "Net Loss" if the expenses exceeded the revenue) at the left margin of the account title column.

16. To determine if the income statement net income or net loss is correct, match it with the net income or net loss shown on the previous worksheet. These figures must match in order to proceed with the financial report process. If the amount matches the net income or net loss on the worksheet, draw a double line across both columns under the amount representing the income or loss. This verifies that the amount is correct.

Lawson's Lawn Care				
Income Statement				
For the Month Ended July 31, 20—				
Revenue:				
Sales			4367	00
Expenses:				
Advertising Expense	86	00		
Insurance Expense	330	00		
Miscellaneous Expense	95	00		
Rent Expense	450	00		
Supplies Expense	1341	00		
Utilities Expense	125	00		
Total Expenses			2427	00	**13**
Net Income **15**			**14** 1940	00	**16**

8

Income Statements With Multiple Revenue Accounts

Most small businesses record all income under one account such as Sales or Fees. However, many business owners prefer to present a more detailed account of their revenue, so they break down their sources of revenue into two or more accounts to give a clearer picture of all sources of revenue from the business.

The income statement shown below (based on the worksheet in Exercise 3.7 in LIFEPAC 5) illustrates how a business with more than one revenue account would list the accounts.

Bob's Boat Rental					
Income Statement					
For the Quarter Ended May 31, 20—					
Revenue:					
Boat Rental	16548	00			
Fishing Equipment Sales	18301	00			
Total Revenue			34849	00	
Expenses:					
Advertising Expense	12165	00			
Insurance Expense	870	00			
Miscellaneous Expense	2158	00			
Rent Expense	6000	00			
Repair Expense	2603	00			
Supplies Expense – Office	742	00			
Supplies Expense – Store	1286	00			
Utilities Expense	2489	00			
Total Expenses			28313	00	
Net Income			6536	00	

Income Statement With a Net Loss

The income statement shown below (based on the worksheet in Exercise 3.6 in LIFEPAC 5) illustrates how a net loss would be recorded.

Fox Photography
Income Statement
For the Quarter Ended March 31, 20—

Revenue:				
Sales				8628 00
Expenses:				
Advertising Expense		2775 00		
Insurance Expense		1400 00		
Miscellaneous Expense		615 00		
Rent Expense		1280 00		
Repair Expense		885 00		
Supplies Expense – Office		1849 00		
Supplies Expense – Store		1000 00		
Utilities Expense		25 00		
Total Expenses				9829 00
Net Loss				1201 00

Use the forms on the next page to complete the following activities.

1.1   Use the following account balances to prepare an income statement for **Holiday Tours** for the month ended March 31 of the current year:

Sales	$1,200.00	Advertising Expense	$ 75.00
Membership Fees	600.00	Miscellaneous Expense	440.00
		Rent Expense	955.00
		Utilities Expense	120.00

1.2   Use the following account balances to prepare an income statement for **Overview Tours** for the month ended July 31 of the current year:

Sales	$1,200.00	Advertising Expense	$ 50.00
		Miscellaneous Expense	150.00
		Rent Expense	450.00
		Utilities Expense	40.00

1.1

1.2

Review the material in this section in preparation for the Self Test. The Self Test will check your mastery of this particular section. The items missed on this Self Test will indicate specific areas where restudy is needed for mastery.

SELF TEST 1

Calculate the net income or net loss (each problem, 3 points).

	Total Revenue	Total Expenses	Net Income	or	Net Loss
1.01	$ 6,000.00	$ 5,500.00	_____		_____
1.02	10,500.00	6,500.00	_____		_____
1.03	2,450.00	875.00	_____		_____
1.04	1,675.00	1,825.00	_____		_____
1.05	21,565.00	16,945.00	_____		_____
1.06	11,850.00	12,250.00	_____		_____
1.07	18,765.00	10,980.00	_____		_____
1.08	22,546.00	19,775.00	_____		_____

Fox Amusement Park
Worksheet
For the Month Ended October 31, 20—

ACCOUNT NAME	TRIAL BALANCE DEBIT	TRIAL BALANCE CREDIT	INCOME STATEMENT DEBIT	INCOME STATEMENT CREDIT	BALANCE SHEET DEBIT	BALANCE SHEET CREDIT
Cash	4580 00				4580 00	
Computer Supplies	5800 00				5800 00	
Repair Equipment	7800 00				7800 00	
Concession Supply Co.		1560 00				1560 00
Jason Fox, Capital		10200 00				10200 00
Jason Fox, Drawing	900 00				900 00	
Admissions Income		11500 00		11500 00		
Concessions Income		2600 00		2600 00		
Advertising Expense	2500 00		2500 00			
Rent Expense	3500 00		3500 00			
Utilities Expense	780 00		780 00			
Totals	25860 00	25860 00	6780 00	14100 00	19080 00	11760 00
Net Income			7320 00			7320 00
			14100 00	14100 00	19080 00	19080 00

12

Complete the following activities.

1.09 Use the worksheet on the previous page to prepare an income statement for **Fox Amusement Park** (24 points total).

1.010 Use the following account balances to prepare an income statement for **Lawrence Landscaping** for the month ended January 31 of the current year (24 points total).

Sales	$28,500.00	Rent Expense	$ 12,000.00
Advertising Expense	9,950.00	Salary Expense	6,000.00
Miscellaneous Expense	165.00	Utilities Expense	1,500.00

58 / 72

Score _____

Adult Check _____

Initial   Date

SECTION II. THE OWNER'S EQUITY STATEMENT

The financial position of a business is shown on two statements—the **statement of owner's equity** and the balance sheet. The statement of owner's equity is prepared first because it is a supporting document that is needed to complete the balance sheet.

At the end of every fiscal period, the balance of the owner's equity account (Capital) must be brought up to date. The financial statement that reports the changes in capital that have occurred between the beginning and ending of a given fiscal period is the statement of owner's equity. By preparing a statement of owner's equity, it is possible to reflect the changes in equity during the fiscal period and the total of the owner's equity at the end of a fiscal period. Net income will increase the value of the capital account, while a net loss will decrease its value. Also, investments by the owner and the owner's withdrawals (Drawing) affect the balance of capital.

The two sources of information to complete a statement of owner's equity are the general ledger Capital account and the worksheet. The six-column worksheet and the Capital account for Overview Tours are illustrated below.

Overview Tours
Worksheet
For the Month Ended July 31, 20—

ACCOUNT NAME	TRIAL BALANCE		INCOME STATEMENT		BALANCE SHEET	
	DEBIT	CREDIT	DEBIT	CREDIT	DEBIT	CREDIT
Cash	24560 00				24560 00	
Petty Cash	300 00				300 00	
Office Equipment	10000 00				10000 00	
Garage Equipment	900 00				900 00	
Staples		450 00				450 00
Town Supply		250 00				250 00
John Jones, Capital		34850 00				34850 00
John Jones, Drawing	300 00				300 00	
Sales		1200 00		1200 00		
Advertising Expense	50 00		50 00			
Miscellaneous Expense	150 00		150 00			
Rent Expense	450 00		450 00			
Utilities Expense	40 00		40 00			
Totals	36750 00	36750 00	690 00	1200 00	36060 00	35550 00
Net Income			510 00			510 00
			1200 00	1200 00	36060 00	36060 00

14

Account Title: *John Jones, Capital*   **Account No.** *310*

Date 20—	Explanation	Post. Ref.	Debit	Credit	Balance Debit	Balance Credit
July 1	Balance Brought Fwd.	✔				32850 00
15		J2		2000 00		34850 00

Statement of Owner's Equity With Additional Investment

Overview Tours
Statement of Owner's Equity
For the Month Ended July 31, 20—

Capital, July 1, 20—		**2**	32850 00
Add: Additional Investments	**3** 2000 00		
Net Income	**4** 510 00		
Net Increase in Capital		**5**	2510 00
Total		**6**	35360 00
Less: Withdrawals		**7**	300 00
John Jones, Capital, July 31, 20—		**8**	35060 00

1. The heading section must provide the name of the business entity, the name of the financial statement and the fiscal period represented (the three W's: *Who*, *What* and *When*).

2. The beginning capital amount for the fiscal period is obtained from the general ledger Capital account and entered in the totals (right) column of the financial statement.

3. List the total of any additional investments made by the owner. This information is also found in the general ledger Capital account.

4. The net income amount for the month of July is obtained from the worksheet and entered in the totals column. A single line is drawn underneath.

5. Add the additional investment and the net income to arrive at the net increase in capital. Place this total in the total column of the statement.

6. Draw a single line under the Net Increase in Capital amount and add this increase to the beginning capital amount to arrive at a subtotal. Enter this amount in the totals column.

7. List the owner's withdrawals (the balance of the Drawing account on the worksheet) in the totals column and draw a single line underneath the amount. Indicate that this amount is to be deducted by writing "Less: Withdrawals."

8. The total brought forward represents the amount of Capital at the end of the fiscal period after increases (additional investments and net income) have been added and decreases (owner's withdrawals) have been deducted. Rule a double line across both columns.

Statement of Owner's Equity Without Additional Investment

If no additional investments of capital were made by the owner during the fiscal period, the statement of owner's equity would look like the example shown below. Note that all amounts are written in the totals column because there is only one entry each for additional income and withdrawals. The list column is used to subtotal *multiple* items of income and/or withdrawals.

Account Title: *John Jones, Capital*								Account No. *310*	
Date 20—		Explanation	Post. Ref.	Debit		Credit		Balance	
								Debit	Credit
July	*1*	*Balance Brought Fwd.*	✔						*34850 00*

Overview Tours
Statement of Owner's Equity
For the Month Ended July 31, 20—

Capital, July 1, 20—			*34850 00*
Add: Net Income			*510 00*
Total			*35360 00*
Less: Withdrawals			*300 00*
John Jones, Capital, July 31, 20—			*35060 00*

Statement of Owner's Equity with Net Loss

If a business has a net loss, a decrease in capital would be shown on the statement of owner's equity. The statement shown below for Fox Photography (based on the worksheet in Exercise 3.6 in LIFEPAC 5) illustrates how a net loss would appear.

Fox Photography
Statement of Owner's Equity
For the Month Ended March 31, 20—

Capital, March 1, 20—			12585	00
Less: Net Loss	1201	00		
Withdrawals	1560	00		
Net Decrease in Capital			2761	00
Mike Fox, Capital, March 31, 20—			9824	00

Statement of Owner's Equity with Additional Investment and Net Loss

Account Title: *John Jones, Capital*   **Account No.** *310*

Date 20—		Explanation	Post. Ref.	Debit		Credit		Balance Debit		Balance Credit	
July	1	Balance Brought Fwd.	✔							32850	00
	15		G2			2000	00			34850	00

Overview Tours
Statement of Owner's Equity
For the Month Ended July 31, 20—

Capital, July 1, 20—			32850	00
Add: Additional Investment			2000	00
Total			34850	00
Less: Net Loss	640	00		
Withdrawals	300	00		
Net Decrease in Capital			940	00
John Jones, Capital, July 31, 20—			33910	00

Complete the following activities.

2.1   Complete a statement of owner's equity for **Bob's Boat Rental**, owned by Robert
       Borden, for the quarter ended May 31 of the current year. Use the following informa-
       tion:

Balance of Capital account on March 1	$17,688.00
Additional investment of capital	1,000.00
Withdrawals by owner	2,590.00
Net Income	6,536.00

2.2   Complete a statement of owner's equity for **Donald Frost, M.D.** for the quarter ended
       September 30 of the current year. Use the following information:

Balance of Capital account on July 1	$23,514.00
Withdrawals by owner	8,560.00
Net Income	8,623.00

2.3   Complete a statement of owner's equity for **Lawson's Travel Agency**, owned by Rachel Lawson, for the month ended June 30 of the current year. Use the following information:

Balance of Capital account on June 1	$26,390.00
Withdrawals by owner	900.00
Net Loss	1,180.00

2.4   Complete a statement of owner's equity for **Joe Blow's Duct Cleaning Service**, owned by Joseph Blow, for the month ended April 30 of the current year. Use the following information:

Balance of Capital account on April 1	$15,000.00
Additional investment of capital	2,500.00
Withdrawals by owner	750.00
Net Loss	2,375.00

Review the material in this section in preparation for the Self Test. This Self Test will check your mastery of this particular section as well as your knowledge of the previous section.

SELF TEST 2

Calculate the ending capital balance, then use the accounting equation *(Assets = Liabilities + Capital)* to prove the accuracy of the ending capital amount (each answer, 1 point).

	Total Assets	Total Liabilities	Total Capital	Total Drawing	Net Income or (Net Loss)	Ending Capital Balance
2.01	$ 3,158.00	$1,228.00	$1,580.00	$ 800.00	$1,150.00	_____
	_____ =	_____	_____ +	_____		
2.02	6,659.00	2,860.00	3,990.00	1,680.00	1,489.00	_____
	_____ =	_____	_____ +	_____		
2.03	4,527.00	1,755.00	1,987.00	200.00	985.00	_____
	_____ =	_____	_____ +	_____		
2.04	2,094.00	1,575.00	1,199.00	500.00	(180.00)	_____
	_____ =	_____	_____ +	_____		
2.05	11,335.00	3,270.00	7,000.00	195.00	1,260.00	_____
	_____ =	_____	_____ +	_____		
2.06	7,759.00	5,250.00	3,690.00	895.00	(286.00)	_____
	_____ =	_____	_____ +	_____		
2.07	7,790.00	2,610.00	3,960.00	220.00	1,440.00	_____
	_____ =	_____	_____ +	_____		
2.08	18,540.00	9,880.00	7,890.00	1,200.00	1,970.00	_____
	_____ =	_____	_____ +	_____		

Johnson's Computer Service
Worksheet
For the Month Ended December 31, 20—

ACCOUNT NAME	TRIAL BALANCE DEBIT	TRIAL BALANCE CREDIT	INCOME STATEMENT DEBIT	INCOME STATEMENT CREDIT	BALANCE SHEET DEBIT	BALANCE SHEET CREDIT
Cash	2580 00				2580 00	
Computer Supplies	800 00				800 00	
Delivery Equipment	10600 00				10600 00	
Repair Equipment	7800 00				7800 00	
Computer Supply Co.		6560 00				6560 00
Kellie Johnson, Capital		19200 00				19200 00
Kellie Johnson, Drawing	1900 00				1900 00	
Computer Sales		11500 00		11500 00		
Repair Income		11500 00		11500 00		
Advertising Expense	12500 00		12500 00			
Miscellaneous Expense	1200 00		1200 00			
Rent Expense	9600 00		9600 00			
Utilities Expense	1780 00		1780 00			
Totals	48760 00	48760 00	25080 00	23000 00	23680 00	25760 00
Net Loss				2080 00	2080 00	
			25080 00	25080 00	25760 00	25760 00

Use the worksheet on the previous page to prepare an income statement for Johnson's Computer Service (27 points total).

2.09

Use the worksheet on the previous page to prepare a statement of owner's equity for Johnson's Computer Service. There were no additional investments (16 points total).

2.010

Score _____

Adult Check _____

Initial   Date

SECTION III. THE BALANCE SHEET

Balance Sheet Formats

Along with the statement of owner's equity, the balance sheet shows the financial position of a business at the end of a fiscal period.

Account Format. There are two forms of balance sheets. You are already familiar with the **account format** which lists the assets on the left and the liabilities and capital on the right, as shown below:

Burke's Bagels Balance Sheet June 30, 20–					
Assets			**Liabilities**		
Cash	1400	00	Accounts Payable 1100.00		
Accounts Receivable	600	00	Notes Payable 700.00		
Supplies	1400	00	Total Liabilities	1800	00
Prepaid Insurance	500	00			
Equipment	2600	00	**Capital**		
			Buford Burke, Capital	4700	00
Total Assets	6500	00	Total Liabilities & Capital	6500	00

Report Format. The **report format** balance sheet is the most common balance sheet format. It lists the assets section first, followed by the liabilities section, then the owner's equity section. This is a two-column report format similar to the income statement.

ACCOUNTING

six

LIFEPAC TEST

95 / 119

Name _____

Date _____

Score _____

LIFEPAC TEST ACCOUNTING 6

PART I

On the blank, print a *T* if the statement is true or an *F* if the statement is false (each correct answer, 1 point).

1. _____ A major function of a worksheet is to assist in planning and preparing financial statements.

2. _____ The statement that reports the financial condition of a business on a specific date is the income statement.

3. _____ Matching expenses with revenue is the accounting concept applied when preparing an income statement at the end of a fiscal period.

4. _____ The statement that reports the financial condition of a business on a specific date is the balance sheet.

5. _____ Single lines ruled across the amount columns of any statement indicate that those amounts are accurate and correct.

6. _____ To prepare an income statement, the information is obtained from the worksheet's account title and trial balance columns.

7. _____ The report format of the balance sheet lists the assets on the left and the liabilities and equity on the right.

8. _____ The owner's equity statement is the connecting link between the income statement and the balance sheet.

9. _____ All financial statements have the same heading, listing the name of the business entity, the name of the statement and date of the statement.

10. _____ The account format of the balance sheet lists the assets on the left and the liabilities and equity on the right.

11. _____ Net income occurs when expenses are greater than revenue.

12. _____ Double lines drawn underneath the net income figure on an income statement indicate that the figure is verified as correct.

13. _____ The owner's equity statement shows the owner's share of the business assets.

14. _____ Consistent reporting requires that the business use the same accounting procedures from one fiscal period to the next.

15. _____ The owner's equity statement lists the changes in capital from the beginning to the end of a fiscal period.

For each statement below, circle the letter of the choice that best completes the sentence (each answer, 1 point).

16. The net income reported on the income statement should be the same as:
    a. shown on a worksheet
    b. shown on the balance sheet
    c. shown on the last income statement
    d. shown in the owner's equity account

17. The account balances needed to complete an income statement are obtained from the worksheet's:
    a. trial balance columns
    b. general ledger accounts
    c. income statement columns
    d. balance sheet columns

18. The account balances needed to complete a balance sheet are obtained from the worksheet's:
    a. trial balance columns
    b. general ledger accounts
    c. income statement columns
    d. balance sheet columns

19. Income statement figures are considered to be correct when:
    a. the income statement balances
    b. the net income or net loss agrees with the worksheet
    c. the owner's equity is the same
    d. the last line representing the net income figure is double ruled

20. The formula for determining owner's equity is:
    a. beginning capital plus net income minus withdrawals by the owner
    b. beginning capital minus net income plus withdrawals by the owner
    c. use the Capital account balance listed on the worksheet
    d. use the balance from the Drawing account in the general ledger

21. The balance sheet is considered complete and accurate when:
    a. amounts on the worksheet and the balance sheet agree
    b. beginning capital plus net income equals ending capital
    c. the total assets equal the total liabilities and owner's equity

22. A net loss occurs when:
    a. total revenue is greater than total expenses
    b. the capital account is larger than the net income
    c. total expenses are greater than total revenue
    d. the cash account has no balance

2

23. A net income occurs when:
    a. total revenue is greater than total expenses
    b. the capital account is larger than the net income
    c. total expenses are greater than total revenue
    d. the cash account has no balance

24. The balance sheet shows the financial condition of a business:
    a. for the entire fiscal period
    b. on a specific date
    c. for a year
    d. on the date of organization

25. The income statement shows the financial progress of a business:
    a. for the entire fiscal period
    b. on a specific date
    c. for a year
    d. on the date of organization

26. The body of an income statement is comprised of:
    a. assets, liabilities and equity
    b. the who, what and when of the statement
    c. revenue, expenses and net income/net loss
    d. beginning capital, net income and ending capital

27. To complete the asset section of a balance sheet, the figures are obtained from the worksheet's:
    a. trial balance debit column
    b. income statement debit column
    c. balance sheet debit column
    d. balance sheet credit column

28. To complete the liability section of a balance sheet, the figures are obtained from the worksheet's:
    a. trial balance debit column
    b. income statement debit column
    c. balance sheet debit column
    d. balance sheet credit column

29. To complete the revenue section of an income statement, the figures are obtained from the worksheet's:
    a. balance sheet debit column
    b. income statement debit column
    c. income statement credit column
    d. balance sheet credit column

30. To complete the expense section of an income statement, the figures are obtained from the worksheet's:
    a. balance sheet debit column
    b. income statement debit column
    c. income statement credit column
    d. balance sheet credit column

31. The last section of an income statement is:
    a. total revenue
    b. total expenses
    c. total owner's equity
    d. net income or net loss

32. The balance of the owner's capital account shown on the worksheet represents:
    a. the balance at the beginning of the fiscal period
    b. the balance at the end of the fiscal period
    c. the original investment by the owner
    d. the cash account balance

33. The major goal of every business entity is:
    a. to make a profit
    b. to operate at a loss
    c. to borrow operating capital
    d. to go bankrupt

34. The owner's equity statement shows the changes in capital that occur:
    a. for the entire fiscal period
    b. on a specific date
    c. for a year
    d. date of organization

35. All financial statements are required to have a heading. This heading consists of:
    a. assets, liabilities and capital
    b. revenue, expenses and net income/net loss,
    c. name of the entity, name of the statement and date of the statement
    d. beginning capital, withdrawals and ending capital

PART II

Shown below is a partial worksheet for **The Hartman Company** prepared on November 30 of the current year (84 points total).

Instructions:

1. Prepare an **income statement** on the form provided.

2. Prepare a **statement of owner's equity** on the form provided. The owner made an additional investment of $1,500.00. NOTE: This amount needs to be *subtracted* from the balance of the owner's capital account on the worksheet to arrive at the balance for John Hartman, Capital as of November 1 of the current year.

3. Prepare a **balance sheet** on the form provided.

The Hartman Company
Worksheet
For the Month Ended November 30, 20—

ACCOUNT NAME	INCOME STATEMENT		BALANCE SHEET	
	DEBIT	CREDIT	DEBIT	CREDIT
Cash			3900 00	
Petty Cash			300 00	
Office Supplies			2700 00	
Store Supplies			3700 00	
Prepaid Insurance			1400 00	
Black's Insurance Co.				1100 00
Staples Office Supply				650 00
Thomas Hartman, Capital				10410 00
Thomas Hartman, Drawing			950 00	
Commissions		5200 00		
Advertising Expense	290 00			
Insurance Expense	500 00			
Miscellaneous Expense	480 00			
Rent Expense	1800 00			
Supplies Expense – Office	560 00			
Supplies Expense – Store	440 00			
Utilities Expense	340 00			
Totals	4410 00	5200 00	12950 00	12160 00
Net Income	790 00			790 00
	5200 00	5200 00	12950 00	12950 00

Income statement:

Statement of owner's equity:

Balance sheet:

The information for the following statement of owner's equity and balance sheet for **Clever Closet Company** is taken from the worksheet in Exercise 2.1 of LIFEPAC 5.

Clever Closet Company
Statement of Owner's Equity
For the Month Ended October 31, 20—

Capital, October 1, 20—			15000 00
Add: Net Income			455 00
Total			15455 00
Less: Withdrawals			860 00
Joanne Clever, Capital, October 31, 20—		6	14595 00

1 Clever Closet Company
Balance Sheet
October 31, 20—

2 Assets			
Cash	13321 00		
Petty Cash	300 00		
Supplies 3	2200 00		
Prepaid Insurance	900 00		
Total Assets 4		16721 00	
5 Liabilities			
Tyson Office Supply	1166 00		
Office Systems, Inc.	960 00		
Total Liabilities		2126 00	
6 Owner's Equity			
Joanne Clever, Capital		14595 00	
Total Liabilities and Owner's Equity 7		16721 00	

1. The heading section must provide the name of the business entity, the name of the financial statement and the fiscal period represented (the three W's: *Who*, *What* and *When*).

2. Center the word "Assets" on the first line of the account title column.

3. Use the balance sheet section of the worksheet to find the asset account balances to enter in the list column. Rule and total the asset account balances and extend the total assets to the totals column, as shown above.

4. Indent the words "Total Assets" approximately five spaces and rule a double line across both columns under the amount of total assets.

5. Skip a line and prepare the liabilities section in the same manner, using the information found on the balance sheet section of the worksheet. NOTE: Do *not* double rule under the total liabilities amount.

6. Skip a line and center the words "Owner's Equity." Use the information from the owner's statement of equity to enter the updated amount of capital for the business at the close of the fiscal period.

7. Rule and add the liabilities and capital totals and compare that amount to the total assets (Assets = Liabilities + Capital). If the two amounts are equal, double rule across both columns to show that the balance sheet is accurate and complete.

Hints:

1. In order to prove the accuracy of the owner's equity statement, subtract the total liabilities from the total assets and the amount will equal the ending Capital account balance.

2. The income statement and the owner's equity statement provide financial information for the entire fiscal period. Note that the headings on both statements say "For the Month Ended…."

3. The balance sheet reports financial information as of the last day of the fiscal period. Note that a specific date is shown in the heading of the balance sheet.

4. Normally all financial reports are typewritten or computer-generated. If they are handwritten, they should be completed neatly and in ink.

Complete the following activity.

3.1 From the information provided on the following worksheet and statement of owner's equity for **Overview Tours**, prepare a report-style balance sheet dated the last day of the fiscal period. Use the form on the following page.

Overview Tours

Worksheet

For the Month Ended July 31, 20—

ACCOUNT NAME	TRIAL BALANCE		INCOME STATEMENT		BALANCE SHEET	
	DEBIT	CREDIT	DEBIT	CREDIT	DEBIT	CREDIT
Cash	24560 00				24560 00	
Petty Cash	300 00				300 00	
Office Equipment	10000 00				10000 00	
Garage Equipment	900 00				900 00	
Staples		450 00				450 00
Town Supply		250 00				250 00
John Jones, Capital		34850 00				34850 00
John Jones, Drawing	300 00				300 00	
Sales		1200 00		1200 00		
Advertising Expense	50 00		50 00			
Miscellaneous Expense	150 00		150 00			
Rent Expense	450 00		450 00			
Utilities Expense	40 00		40 00			
Totals	36750 00	36750 00	690 00	1200 00	36060 00	35550 00
Net Income			510 00			510 00
			1200 00	1200 00	36060 00	36060 00

Overview Tours

Statement of Owner's Equity

For the Month Ended July 31, 20—

Capital, July 1, 20—			32850	00
Add: Additional Investments	2000	00		
Net Income	510	00		
Net Increase in Capital			2510	00
Total			35360	00
Less: Withdrawals			300	00
John Jones, Capital, July 31, 20—			35060	00

Review the material in this section in preparation for the Self Test. This Self Test will check your mastery of this particular section as well as your knowledge of the previous sections.

SELF TEST 3

Match the following accounting terms with their definitions (each answer, 2 points).

3.01 _____ a report format that lists the assets on the left and the liabilities and equity on the right

      a. account format

3.02 _____ when total expenses exceed total revenue

      b. balance sheet

3.03 _____ shows the financial position of a business on a specific date

      c. fiscal period

3.04 _____ a columnar accounting form used to summarize general ledger information needed to prepare financial reports

      d. income statement

3.05 _____ the financial statement that reports the changes in capital during a fiscal period

      e. net income

3.06 _____ when total revenue exceeds total expenses

      f. net loss

3.07 _____ a report format that lists the assets first, followed by the liabilities and capital

      g. report format

3.08 _____ the length of the accounting cycle for which a business summarizes and reports financial data

      h. statement of owner's equity

      i. net

3.09 _____ reports the revenue, expenses and net income or net loss of a business

      j. worksheet

Complete the following activities:

3.010   Use the account information below to prepare an income statement for the **Miller Company** for the month ended April 30 of the current year (26 points total).

Sales	$1,900.00	Miscellaneous Expense	$ 75.00
		Rent Expense	450.00
Advertising Expense	50.00	Repair Expense	95.00
Insurance Expense	110.00	Utilities Expense	285.00

Floor-Shine Company
Worksheet
For the Month Ended November 30, 20—

ACCOUNT TITLE	TRIAL BALANCE		ADJUSTMENTS		INCOME STATEMENT		BALANCE SHEET	
	DEBIT	CREDIT	DEBIT	CREDIT	DEBIT	CREDIT	DEBIT	CREDIT
Cash	5844 00						5844 00	
Petty Cash	300 00						300 00	
Supplies	1900 00			(a) 600 00			1300 00	
Prepaid Insurance	800 00			(b) 400 00			400 00	
Tyson Office Supply		166 00						166 00
Office Systems, Inc.		60 00						60 00
Mike Ford, Capital		8000 00						8000 00
Mike Ford, Drawing	560 00						560 00	
Sales		1628 00				1628 00		
Advertising Expense	75 00				75 00			
Insurance Expense			(b) 400 00		400 00			
Miscellaneous Expense	15 00				15 00			
Rent Expense	250 00				250 00			
Repair Expense	85 00				85 00			
Supplies Expense			(a) 600 00		600 00			
Utilities Expense	25 00				25 00			
Totals	9854 00	9854 00	1000 00	1000 00	1450 00	1628 00	8404 00	8226 00
Net Income					178 00			178 00
					1628 00	1628 00	8404 00	8404 00

3.011 Use the account information on the above worksheet to prepare a statement of owner's equity for the **Floor-Shine Company**. There were no additional investments (16 total points).

28

3.012 Use the information on the worksheet on the previous page to prepare a balance sheet for the **Floor-Shine Company** dated the last day of the fiscal period (31 total points).

73 / 91

Score _____

Adult Check _____

Initial   Date

SECTION IV. REVIEW & APPLICATION PROBLEMS

Prepare an income statement.

4.1   Using the partial worksheet below, prepare an income statement for the **Skate-O-Rama Company**. Use the form on the next page.

Skate-O-Rama Company
Worksheet
For the Month Ended November 30, 20—

ACCOUNT NAME	INCOME STATEMENT	
	DEBIT	CREDIT
Membership Fees		6850 00
Rental Fees		2290 00
Advertising Expense	650 00	
Insurance Expense	910 00	
Miscellaneous Expense	475 00	
Rent Expense	1600 00	
Repair Expense	995 00	
Salary Expense	1800 00	
Supplies Expense	1285 00	
Totals	7715 00	9140 00
Net Income	1425 00	
	9140 00	9140 00

Prepare an income statement.

4.2   Use the following accounts and their balances to complete this activity:

Auto Repair Income	$ 6,122.00	Advertising Expense	$ 1,812.00
Auto Parts Income	4,077.00	Insurance Expense	1,922.00
		Miscellaneous Expense	275.00
		Rent Expense	1,800.00
		Repair Expense	1,095.00
		Salary Expense	2,800.00
		Supplies Expense	1,480.00

a. Calculate the net income or net loss for the fiscal period: _____

b. Prepare an income statement for **Smith's Garage** for the month ended July 31 of the current year.

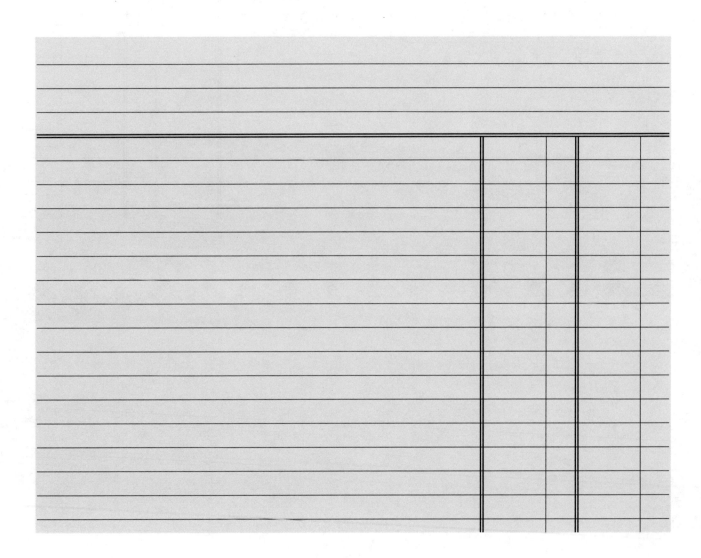

Complete these activities.

4.3   Complete a statement of owner's equity for **Golf-A-Rama** for the month ended
December 31 of the current year. Use the following information:

Balance of Capital account on December 1	$25,000.00
Additional investment	4,000.00
Net Income	7,250.00
Withdrawals by the owner, Bradley Stevens	2,600.00

4.4   Complete a statement of owner's equity for the **Miller Muffin Company** for the month
ended September 30 of the current year. Use the following information:

Balance of Capital account on September 1	$22,000.00
Net Income	8,500.00
Withdrawals by the owner, Melvin Miller	2,400.00

Prepare a balance sheet.

4.5 Use the following accounts and their balances to prepare a balance sheet for **Nails by Jane**, owned by Jane Osgood. The business has a monthly fiscal period. This balance sheet will be for the fiscal period ending on September 30 of the current year.

Assets		Liabilities	
Cash	$ 2,685.00	Harrison Beauty Supply	$ 890.00
Petty Cash	200.00	Jones Office Supplies	240.00
Prepaid Insurance	900.00	**Owner's Equity**	
Supplies	240.00	Jane Osgood, Capital	2,895.00

Complete the following activity.

4.6   Classify each account and indicate by a check mark if the account balance will be a debit or credit in the trial balance columns and in which financial statements the balance will be found. The first one has been done for you as an example.

Account Title	Account Classification	Trial Balance		Financial Statements		
		Debit	Credit	Income Statement	Owner's Equity	Balance Sheet
Cash	Asset	✔				✔
Sales						
Petty Cash						
Members' Fees						
Accounts Receivable						
Rent Expense						
Office Supplies						
Miscellaneous Expense						
Prepaid Insurance						
Store Supplies						
Salary Expense						
Sam's Club						
Joe Wilson, Capital						
Commissions						
GMAC Finance						
Joe Wilson, Drawing						
Utilities Expense						

West View Garage
Worksheet
For the Month Ended December 31, 20—

ACCOUNT NAME	TRIAL BALANCE		INCOME STATEMENT		BALANCE SHEET	
	DEBIT	CREDIT	DEBIT	CREDIT	DEBIT	CREDIT
Cash	6284 00				6284 00	
Petty Cash	400 00				400 00	
Prepaid Insurance	1115 00				1115 00	
Office Supplies	250 00				250 00	
Store Supplies	775 00				775 00	
Garage Equipment	9380 00				9380 00	
United Auto Parts		1830 00				1830 00
First City Bank		2020 00				2020 00
Bruce West, Capital		12395 00				12395 00
Bruce West, Drawing	600 00				600 00	
Repair Income		5299 00		5299 00		
Advertising Expense	1280 00		1280 00			
Miscellaneous Expense	680 00		680 00			
Rent Expense	540 00		540 00			
Utilities Expense	240 00		240 00			
Totals	21544 00	21544 00	2740 00	5299 00	18804 00	16245 00
Net Income			2559 00			2559 00
			5299 00	5299 00	18804 00	18804 00

 Complete these activities.

Use the above worksheet for **West View Garage** to complete the following financial reports:

4.7   **Prepare an income statement**.

4.8   **Prepare a statement of owner's equity**. The capital on December 1 was $10,395.00, and an additional $2,000.00 investment was made by the owner.

4.9   **Prepare a balance sheet**.

4.7

4.8

Curly-Do Salon
Worksheet
For the Month Ended May 31, 20—

ACCOUNT NAME	INCOME STATEMENT		BALANCE SHEET	
	DEBIT	CREDIT	DEBIT	CREDIT
Cash			6190 00	
Petty Cash			300 00	
Office Supplies			2500 00	
Store Supplies			3500 00	
Prepaid Insurance			2400 00	
Beauty Supply House				2890 00
Staples Office Supply				565 00
Sue Curly, Capital				12795 00
Sue Curly, Drawing			1050 00	
Personal Care Income		5800 00		
Beauty Products Income		3300 00		
Advertising Expense	290 00			
Insurance Expense	500 00			
Miscellaneous Expense	480 00			
Rent Expense	4800 00			
Supplies Expense – Office	1560 00			
Supplies Expense – Store	1440 00			
Utilities Expense	340 00			
Totals	9410 00	9100 00	15940 00	16250 00
Net Loss		310 00	310 00	
	9410 00	9410 00	16250 00	16250 00

 Complete the following activities.

A partial worksheet for the **Curly-Do Salon** is shown above. On the forms provided on the next two pages, prepare the following reports:

4.10 **Prepare an income statement.**

4.11 **Prepare a statement of owner's equity.** The owner did not make any additional investment.

4.12 **Prepare a balance sheet.**

4.10

4.11

4.12

Complete the following activities.

On April 30 of the current year, **John's Fix-It Shop** has the following general ledger accounts and balances. The business uses a monthly fiscal period.

Assets:

Cash	$ 3,750.00
Petty Cash	100.00
Supplies – Office	1,800.00
Supplies – Parts	1,600.00
Prepaid Insurance	950.00
Equipment	3,775.00

Liabilities & Capital:

Johnson Supply	$ 375.00
Wells Company	900.00
John Goodie, Capital	7,875.00
John Goodie, Drawing	430.00

Revenue:

Parts Sales	$1,975.00
Repair Sales	2,850.00

Expenses:

Advertising Expense	$470.00
Insurance Expense	
Miscellaneous Expense	130.00
Rent Expense	600.00
Supplies Expense – Office	
Supplies Expense – Parts	
Utilities Expense	370.00

Instructions:

4.13 **Complete the worksheet** on the next page.

   a. Prepare the heading and trial balance on the worksheet on the next page.

   b. Calculate the amount of supplies used and insurance expired and record the adjustments on the worksheet:

   > Supplies – Office on hand on April 30: $910.00
   > Supplies – Parts on hand on April 30: $795.00
   > Value of Prepaid Insurance on April 30: $750.00

   c. Extend the updated account balances to the balance sheet and income statement columns, and complete the worksheet.

4.14 **Prepare an income statement**.

4.15 **Prepare a statement of owner's equity**. There were no additional investments.

4.16 **Prepare a balance sheet**.

Worksheet for Exercise 4.13

ACCOUNT NAME	TRIAL BALANCE		ADJUSTMENTS		INCOME STATEMENT		BALANCE SHEET	
	DEBIT	CREDIT	DEBIT	CREDIT	DEBIT	CREDIT	DEBIT	CREDIT

4.14

4.15

44

Extra forms: